PETS

by Claire Watts
Illustrated by Louise Vo

Pets are animals that live with us in our homes. Pets are good company and they are fun to play with. It is important to take good care of pets.

CATS

Cats are friendly animals. They like to sit on people's laps and rub up against them. Cats also like to go out alone.

Cats use their whiskers to feel their way through narrow spaces.

Mother cats pick their kittens up carefully by the loose skin on the scruff of their necks.

When kittens are born, they cannot see. They open their eyes when they are a week old.

DOGS

Dogs make good pets. They are friendly and easy to train.

When they are too hot, dogs stick their tongues out and pant. This helps them to cool down.

Dogs recognise people and things by the way they smell. Dogs can not see as well as people.

Dogs love to be stroked. A mother dog licks her puppies to make them feel safe.

When dogs are pleased to see you they wag their tails. When they are angry the fur on their neck stands on end.

WORKING DOGS

Some dogs are taught to help people. They learn quickly and remember many commands.

Huskies are used to pull sleds in snowy countries.

Rescue workers use St Bernards to help find people who are lost on mountains.

Sheep dogs help farmers to herd sheep.

HAMSTERS

In the wild, hamsters live in the desert. They spend the day sleeping in cool burrows and only come out at night.

Hamsters store food in pouches at the sides of their mouths. They then hide the food in a secret store.

Hamsters have long, curved front teeth which are good for gnawing. They chew hard things to wear these teeth down.

Pet hamsters like to play with toys such as cardboard tubes and rolled up newspaper.

GUINEA PIGS

Guinea pigs come from South America. In the wild, they live in burrows. Guinea pigs like to eat hay, raw vegetables and fruit. They also need a piece of wood to gnaw on.

Guinea pigs like to have company. When the weather is cold, the guinea pigs huddle together to keep themselves warm.

Guinea pigs need a place where they can roam around on the grass, safe from cats and dogs.

Guinea pigs are not really pigs. They come from the same family as hamsters and gerbils.

GERBILS

In the wild, gerbils live in deserts, just like hamsters. Gerbils drink very little. In their desert home there is hardly any water.

When gerbils are frightened, they stand up on their back legs and tap the ground with their feet.

Gerbils have long furry tails, with a hairy tuft at the end. They have pale fur on their stomachs.

Gerbil babies begin to eat grains and seeds when they are three weeks old. The father gerbil helps the mother look after the babies.

RABBITS

Wild rabbits live in groups in grassy places. They build underground burrows which are called warrens.

Rabbits use their strong hind legs to help them hop along. When rabbits are frightened they stamp their feet to warn others of the danger.

Rabbits have long ears which help them hear well.

Female rabbits can have up to 24 babies every year. Baby rabbits are born blind and with no hair.

BUDGIES

Budgies come from the forests of Australia. In the wild, they live in huge flocks.

Male budgies have a blue patch above their beaks. Female budgies have a brown patch.

Many budgies like to take a bath in a saucer of water.

Budgies like to eat seeds and fruit. Two budgies will often pass food to one another.

GOLDFISH

Goldfish should not be kept in bowls with narrow tops. They are more comfortable in large tanks. Some goldfish live until they are fifty years old.

Goldfish are not all orange! They can be red, brown, grey, black and white.

If they live in a pond, goldfish can grow very big. Goldfish which live in tanks are usually quite small.

Goldfish are probably the easiest pets to look after. They need to be fed twice a day and cleaned out every week.

PET QUIZ

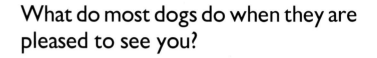

What do most dogs do when they are pleased to see you?

What do cats use their whiskers for?

Where do gerbils live in the wild?

Where do hamsters store their food?

How do guinea pigs keep warm?

What are baby rabbits like when they are born?

Which is the male budgie?

What do sheep dogs help farmers to do?

INDEX

First published in Great Britain in 1991 by
Two-Can Publishing Ltd, 346 Old Street, London EC1V 9NQ

Copyright © Two-Can Publishing Ltd, 1991
Illustrations copyright © Louise Voce, 1991

Printed in Hong Kong

4   6   8   10   9   7   5   3

British Library Cataloguing in Publication Data
Watts, Claire
Pets. - (Jump! starts first look at animals (1))
I. Title II. Series
636.088

PBK ISBN 1-85434-117-0
HBK ISBN 1-85434-127-8

Photo credits:
p. 2-3 Image Bank, p. 5 Ardea, p. 7 Animals Unlimited, p. 9 Marc Henrie, p. 11 NHPA, p. 13 NHPA, p. 15 Bruce Coleman,
p. 17 Image Bank, p. 19 Bruce Coleman, p. 21 Bruce Coleman, back cover Bruce Coleman.